THE GREATEST SACRIFICE

THE GREATEST SACRIFICE

Where Do You Stand?

RICHARD LYONS

authorHOUSE®

AuthorHouse™
1663 Liberty Drive
Bloomington, IN 47403
www.authorhouse.com
Phone: 1-800-839-8640

First published by AuthorHouse   06/24/2011

ISBN: 978-1-4634-1954-7 (sc)
ISBN: 978-1-4634-2284-4 (ebk)

Library of Congress Control Number: 2011909582

Printed in the United States of America

Any people depicted in stock imagery provided by Thinkstock are models, and such images are being used for illustrative purposes only.
Certain stock imagery © Thinkstock.

This book is printed on acid-free paper.

Preface

The volume you hold in your hand represents a collection of topics

put in poetic and biblical form for the enjoyment of all who choose

to read the contents. It is intended to cause some deep and perhaps

some provocative thoughts about the way we live and go about our

daily routines. There may be some comparison poems that you find

amusing and real. It is my hope that your reading and interpretation

causes you much comfort and joy.

Contents

Continued

" Introduction"

Inside , you will find a collection of poetry and prose that you certaintly will enjoy and identify with as you continue your trip to the final conclusion. It includes some possible steps and some inevitable pitfalls that we all are subjected to.It also details what we can and should do, to be redeemed. Also,included are some biblical reflections which serve to pinpoint our memories of some of the happenings in the bible. In addition ,there are some colorful biblical photos that will surely perk your imagination, in regard to ancient times.

Let's face it,we all live in a technologicaly advancing world and staying focused ,plus keeping things prioritized is a real challenge.You see it makes no difference at all about the various prejudices that we use to discriminate. For we all are the same in God's eyesight. So the following pages provide food for thought for all to read.

Although we all may be on a different rating scale when it comes to Sin, our relationship with God is very important. So, enjoy the following pages And: " If you m iss the journey,don't miss the trip". Just renember that all that we do, we could never pay the price, for he gave his son Jesus. He made the greatest sacrifice.

ENJOY!!

" Our Universal God"

Regardless to skin color, ethnicity or race,

It is his total love for us that causes us all to seek his face.

His magnificence is recognized over land and sea

Proven, by the ultimate sacrifice given for you and me

The persistent pleas by his messengers are strong as he gives his heavenly glance,

Shows that he wants to reconcile us all back to him and give man a final chance.

For on judgement day when Jesus returns and the trumpet will sound,

He will separate the good and evil from the worlds training ground.

Made in his own image, we are at the top of the living chain

However, our worship of the flesh over the spirit for him causes much pain.

We must demonstrate our faith, obedience and love,

To prove that we are truly worthy to spend eternity above.

So continuing to spread his name and love by our technology to disperse

Will reach those whose ears are open throughout the universe

By reaching , teaching and continuing to praise his name,

We are continuing to honor his covenant and exalt his fame.

" Soliliquies (Reflections) From God"

Genesis: 1. In the beginning, God created the Heaven and the Earth.

Genesis: 1:5 And God called the light day and the darkness he called night.
and the evening and the morning were the 1ˢᵗ day.

Genesis 1:24. And God said, "Let the earth bring forth the living creature
after his kind: And so it was

.

Genesis 1:27. So God created man In his own image, in the image of God
created he him: Male and Female created he them.

"Understanding God's Plan"

The greatest choice and goal in life that man can achieve

Is a simple commitment for all—" we must first believe"

Being born to a father and mother is easy to understand

However, our cornerstone to eternal life with God, is to be born again

To cast aside all of the idols that the world has to please us

We must continue to stay focused on the one who died for our sins - "Christ Jesus"

Daily reading his word and continuing to understand

He admonishes us to stay true to his precepts and follow his plan

For when God gave his only begotten son, he demonstrated his love

Which was the ultimate gift and sacrifice he could offer from above

His blood was shed for both saint and sinner

Only through him will we become the ultimate winner

God's covenant with us was filled with his passion to forgive

He wants us to forever praise his name and change the way we live

To repent our sins to him and forget the worldly perks

For he wants us to continue to be vigilant and do his Godly works

*Remember, God through his love, gave his son Jesus for you and me

And to be reconciled back to him is the only way to be eternally free.

Richard Lyons

"Soliloquies(Reflections) From God"

Genesis 2: 2. And on the seventh day God ended his work which he had made;

and he rested on the seventh day from all his work.

Genesis 2: 7.And the Lord God formed man of the dust of the ground, and

breathed in his nostrils the breath of life and man became a

living soul.

Genesis 2:8 And the Lord God planted a garden eastward in Eden; and there

he put man who he had formed.

Genesis 2:22. And the rib, which the lord had taken from man, made he a woman,

and brought her unto the man.

A Human Prelude To Eternity

Living life to its' fullest for every human being should be the universal goal

Striving to keep Gods commandments is utmost for the young and the old

To begin every day in humility, thankfulness and seeking guidance is the key

For to understand the fulfillment of life is about God and not about me

To ask for a piggy bank of blessings sprinkled with the value of doing his will

Is to continually be vigilant and expect an abundance only God can fill

So, as we continue to order our steps in your word

Also, cause our voices to be strong and cause your message to be heard

With an abundance of your steadfastness, we can endure the pain

Although trials and tribulation will come, teach us to dance in the rain

With a constant dose of your longsuffering we know that we will be left standing

After all, you never promised us a calm passage, just a safe landing

As we continue our passage, we will keep your message in everything we do

So strengthen our faith , and guide us so that we will make it through

In the meantime, we will offer repentance to overcome our sin

Then, your goal to reconcile us back to you through your son Jesus is a battle we will win

Richard Lyons

"Soliloquies(Reflections) From God"

Genesis 3:3 But the fruit of the tree which is in the midst of the garden, God hath sai

       Ye shall not eat of it, neither shall ye touch it, lest ye die.

Genesis 3:6 And when the woman saw that the tree was good for food, and that it w

       Pleasant to the eyes, and a tree to be desired to make one wise, she took of

       The fruit thereof,and did eat, and gave also unto her husband with her; ar

       He did eat. (Thus The Fall of Man)

" The Power Of Prayer"

To Begin each day with a gesture of humility,

Is to be totally free from stress and lost in total tranquility.

On bending knees with all of my thoughts directed above

I continue my communication with him, in our covenant of love

Although, sometimes I search for the right words when all is still,

I ask for the right guidance and vigilance, because I want to do his will.

For with all of the worldly resistance that I need , with him I want to remain humble

Because, I always want him to pick me up in case I stumble

I confess that as a born sinner, my life is not one of perfection

However, I repent of my sins and ask for his umbrella of protection

Provide me with the strength in the areas that I am weak

Cause me to be able to meet all the worldly challenges in your name, is what I seek.

For I know, that when I am looking for someone who will really care

I don't have to worry, I know you will always be there

So when the day is done and I am walking my last mile

I'll just think of your promises, and put on my heavenly smile

Richard Lyons

"Soliloquies (Reflections) From God

Genesis 6:5 And God saw that the wickedness of man was great in the earth,

> *and every imagination of the thoughts of the heart was only evil*

> *continually.*

ɭ

Genesis 6:6 And it repented the Lord that he had made man on the earth and

> *It grieved him at his heart.*

Genesis 6:7 And the lord said, " I will destroy man whom I have created from the

> *face of the earth; both man, and beast and the creeping thing, and the fow*

> *of the air for it repententh me that I have made them.*

" A Daily Prescription From God"

Begin every day with a dose of humility on your knees

For to show that you are humble, is sure to please

Giving thanks for the opportunity to talk with me and communicate

Will surely begin the healing process, as you meditate

With the presence of me at work as your smile shines through

You begin to show the world that you have faith inside of you

Although the doctors medication is what they periodically prescribe each day

It is my daily healing hand that causes recovery in every way

Don't let your worries get the best of you

Remember, even Moses started out as a basket case too

Always lift your hand in praise to me every day

And I will surely acknowledge you in every way

So regardless of all the busy activity that goes on around you every day

Just continue to stay focused on hevenly meditation each and every day

Although the pain in your body may cause you to feel blue

Continuously, let it flow through your mind that "I will never leave you"

Richard Lyons

"Soliloquies (Reflections) Of God"

Genesis 6:8 Now, Noah found grace in the eyes of the Lord.

Genesis 6: 13. And God said unto Noah, The end of all flesh is come before me.

for the earth is filled with violence through them; and behold

I will destroy them with the earth.

Genesis 6: 14. Make thee an ark of gopher wood; rooms that thou make in the
**

Ark, and shall pitch it within and without with pitch.

Genasis 6: 19 And of every living thing of all flesh, two of every sort shalt thou

Bring into the ark to keep them alive with thee; they shall be male and

female.

" The Atonement Of Sin"

When God created Adam And Eve To begin

They Proved disobedient and open to sin

While being born to live in this world of temptation

We have been extremely vulnerable since our creation

Although we in this world, think that we have the key to successful living

We don't seem to have conquered the art of forgiving

With our worldly focus and our worship of idols of today

Our daily temptation to sin, occurs in every way

With the constant technology of man, we loose track of " Him"

And in the worldly scramble, we try to keep up with "T HEM"

However, in your covenant of compassion,you say that you will forgive

Admonishing us to repent and turn to you so that we may eternally live

You, through your word, continue to remind us of your final conclusion

So ,we will make truthful amends daily to escape the ultimate confusion

Giving thanks to you for your compassion to forgive our sin

It is our ultimate and humble prayer to you, that will cause us to win

Richard Lyons

"Soliloquies (Reflections) Of God

Genesis 7: 10 And it came to pass after seven days that the waters of the flood were

upon the earth.

Genesis 7: 12 And the rain was upon the earth forty day and forty nights

Genesis 7: 21 And all the flesh died that moved upon the earth, both of

fowl and cattle ,and of beast, and of every creeping thing

that creepeth upon the earth, and every man.

Genesis :7 23 And every living substance was destroyed which was on the

face of the ground,both man and cattle and the creeping

things and the fowls of the heaven; and Noah only remained

alive. And they that were with him in the ark.

Genesis 7:24 And the waters prevailed on the earth an hundred and fifty days.

Genesis 8:1 And God remembered Noah , and every living thing, and all

the cattle that was with him in the ark: and God made a wind to pass

over the earth, and the weters asswaged.

"The Real Challenge of Life"

While being born into this confusing world of strife

It is difficult to uncover the " The Real Challenge in life"

While we should explore the real reason for our creation

We get lost because we live in such a blessed nation

We grow up thinking we should gather all we can and ignore the needy

However, to continue to live like that in God's eyesight, is greedy

Amid Adolescence,peer competition and our addiction to the cell

Will only give us another idol, and send us closer to hell

To become more proficient in his word, God admonishes us to explore

He wants us also to be more charitable to others, and not ignore

Also to be more attentive to his commandments and to avoid sin

But to be repentive to him if we really want to win

While for us ,the accumulation of things seem to be an absolute must

We ignore or leave out the heavenly phrase " I N God we Trust"

Meanwhile, we muddle along each day as we try to make it through

Still, "The real challenge in life" for us all, is to develop our relationship with you

Richard Lyons

13

Soliloquies (Refllections) Of God

Genesis 8:13 And it came to pass in the six hundredth and first year

in the first month, the first day of the month, the waters

were dried up from off the earth ; and Noah removed the

covering of the ark, and looked, and behold, the face of the

ground was dry.

Genesis 9: 1 And God blessed Noah and his sons and said unto them,

"Be fruitful and multiply, and replenish the earth"

Genesis 9: 12 And God said , " This is the token of the covenent which

I make between me and you and every living creature that

Is with you, for perpetual generations.

" God's Heavenly Commands"

" Man's Earthly Plans"

When God initially said "Thou shall have no other gods before me",

He speaks of his jealously of worldly idols on earth, land and sea.

However, with man's brain and his ability to create,

We Continues to produce and worship other images which serve to seal our fate.

He also said that we should not "Take the lord thy God in vain",

Thus, our thoughts of removing his name from our schools and currency causes pain.

Although he commands us to " Honor our father and mother",

As the young quickly grow up, they also disrespect their brother.

One of the visible commandments is "Thou Shall Not Kill",

However, this is widely disregarded, for on a worldwide basis, we seen to get a thrill.

We draw up our own rules and even some of these seem very hollow,

We even invade other countries, give them instructions, and expect them to follow.

He also admonishes us that "Thou Shall Not Steal"

But we use words like confiscate to camaflauge, but our intent is real.

No matter what we do, we disobey as we try to show the world our skill,

When we ultimately covet our neighbors possessions, it is not God's will.

Richard Lyons

Exodus 20:3 Thou shalt have no other Gods before Me.

Exodus 20:4 Thou shalt not make unto thee any graven images,

or any likeness of any thing that is in heaven above,

or is in the earth beneath, or in the water under the earth:

Exodus 20:7 Thou shalt not take the name of the Lord thy God in vain.

Exodus 20:8 Remember the Sabbath day and keep it holy.

Exodus 20:12 Honour thy Father and thy Mother: that thy days may

long upon the land which the Lord thy God giveth.

Exodus 20: 13. Thou shalt not kill.

Exodus 20:14 Thou shalt commit adultery.

Exodus 20: 15 Thou shalt not steal.

Exodus 20: 16 Thou shalt not bear false witness against thy neighbour.

Exodus 20: 17 Thy shall not covet thy neighbour's house, thou shall

not covet thy neighbour's wife , nor his manservant

nor his maidservant, nor his ox, nor his ass, nor any

thing that is thy neighbour's.

Message Of Comfort

The early and resounding message from God is Love and Charity

But , as we live in this world, these traits are a rarity

As we continue live out our lives in doubt and tribulation

Let us not forget the one who is responsible for our very creation

Most of us are content to strive for worldly acceptance every day

However, we only get true satisfaction and peace when doing things Gods' way

Let us continue to stay plugged in and in touch with him who is able

For it is only through him that our lives will be stable

Our lives here on this earth provides Gods' ultimate test

It is not meant to spark human competition nor accumulate the worlds best

And although early in life we were nurtured by a father and a mother

We are continually admonished by God to be charitable and to love our brother

Yes, every day we are bombarded with a world full of deceit and confusion

Still Your word regularly reminds us of your commandments and the final conclusion

Although the battle is yours, we who believe are soldiers in the fight

Continue to equip us with the weapons we need as we walk bravely in your light

Richard Lyons

" The Soliloquies (Reflections) Of God

Psalm : 23: 1 The Lord is my shepard ; I shall not want.

Psalm 23:2 He maketh me to lie down in green pastures:

he leadeth me beside the still waters.

Psalm 23:3 He restoreth my soul: he leadeth me in the path of

righteousness for his name sake.

Psalm 23: 4 Yea, though I walk through the valley of the shadow of death, I will fear

no evil for thy rod and thy staff they comfort me.

Psalm 23:5 Thou preparest a table before me in the presence of mine enemies:

thou anointest my head with oil; my cup runneth over.

Psalm 23:6 Surely goodness and mercy shall follow me all the days of

my life and I will dwell in the house of the Lord forever .

"Our Journey With Jesus"

When we begin our trip with Jesus, we must submit to a plan,

Yes, we must repent and commit to be born again.

Then, with humble humility, it's like starting on the floor,

For us to ever see God he says, that only he is the door.

In him, he wants us to daily abide

Because the journey with him is like no other ride.

With trials, tribulations and an abundance of strife,

There will be a constant battle with satan throughout life.

Although our relationship with him looms more important each day,

We stumble and fall, and sometimes lose our way.

Still, he picks us up and continues to admonish us not to sin,

So we repent to him , he forgives us and we start all over again.

Sometimes, as we travel, we manipulate things in order to please us,

To be successful on our journey however, we must obey Jesus,

The travel station that we encounter in life, will be sprinkled with sin,

However, if we stay the course, continue our course with him, we will certaintly win.

Richard Lyons

" The Soliloquies (Reflections) Of God"

Luke 19: 28 Then when he had thus spoken, he went before, ascending up to
Jerusalem .

Luke 19: 29 And it came to pass, when he was come nigh to Bethpage and
Bethany, at the mount called the Mount of Olives, he sent two of
his disciples.

Luke 19:30 Saying: Go ye into the village over against you; as te enter ,ye shall find
A colt tied, whereon yet never man sat: loose him, and bring him hither.

Luke 19:31 And if any man ask you ,why do you loose him ? thus shall ye say unto
him, because the Lord hath need of him.

Luke 19:35 And they brought him to Jesus: and they cast their garments upon the co
and they sat Jesus thereon,

Luke 19 :37 And was come nigh, even now at the descent of the mount of olives, the
whole multitude of the disciples began to rejoice and praise God with
loud voice for all of the mighty works that they had seen.

"A Sinner, But Still A Soldier"

Whether you be a professional technician or a simple farmer,

To be a fighter for God, we need the full protection of armor.

For once you are identified by Satan, he will challenge your fate,

So, to fight off his constant attacks, we need the full breastplate.

Although in this world we have all sinned and not done things right,

To make the commitment to God, we must be ready for the fight.

Staying true to his precepts and understanding our very creation,

We must fight daily with our vigilant sword and helmet of salvation.

However, although we have to fight, we must still remain humble,

For warding off all of the satanistic attacks, we still may stumble.

But continuing to take up arms is our way to thank you for your intercession,

Because we know that only through you , can we repent our confession.

And finally we realize that fighting for your cause is our only way to show,

That we are ready for your cleasing " To be washed as clean as snow".

Yes, we will continue to be your sheep, and continue to be your cattle,

So continue to equip us with the necessary weapons we need to fight your battle.

Richard Lyons

Matthew 26: 20 Now when the even was come, he sat down with the twelve.

Matthew 26: 21 And as they did eat , he said, Verily I say unto you ,that one

        of you shall betray me.

Matthew26: 22 And they were exceedingly sorrowful , and asked Lord is it I?

Matthew 26: 23 And he answered and said, " He that dippeth his hand with

        me in the dish , the same shall betray me".

Matthew 26 :24 The son of man goeth as it is written of him ; but woe unto that man

        by whom the son of man is betrayed! It had been good for that man

        If he had not been born.

Matthew 26:25 Then Judas, which betrayed him, answered him and said Master

        Is it I ? He said unto him, Thou hast said.

Matthew 26:26 And as they were eating , Jesus took bread, and blessed it, and brake

        then gave it to his disciples and said " Take, eat : this is my body"

Matthew 26:27 And he took the cup, and gave thanks, and gave it to them, saying

        " Drink ye all of it"

Matthew 26 :28 For this is my blood of the new testament, which is shed for many

        for the remission of sins.

" To Explore or Ignore ?"

On a universal basis, we continue our ventures in space,

Even this seems to be competition between the countries to see who will win the race.

Our build up of nuclear weapons seems to be vast,

Still, as the stockpile continues, we have become very skeptical and weary of the blast.

Nationally, we want others to look at us as the best,

As we continue to set the standard for all of the rest.

However, our standards sometimes they don't want to include

Then, do we often times get overly aggressive, and begin to intrude?

Even when some humans leaders show brotherly love with competency and taste,

Do we downplay, demean, or dismiss the direction all because of his race?

It seems that as human beings, it is very hard to please us,

However God says in his word that we should seek the mind of his son, Jesus.

Whether, individually a person is protestant, catholic or some other affiliation,

Should not his choice be respected, regardless of his denomination?

The commands and standards set by Christ are outlined in his word,

Regaredless of our views, it is his beckoning pleas that should be heard.

Richard Lyons

" The Soliloquies (Reflections) Of God

Luke 10: 30 Then Jesus answering said, A certain man went down from Jerusalem to Jericho, and fell among thieves. Which stripped him of his raiment and wounded him, and departed, leaving him half dead.

Luke 10 :31 And by chance there came down a certain preist that way: and when when he saw him, he passed by on the other side.

Luke 10:32 And likewise a Levite, when he was at the place, came and looked on him, and passed by on the other side.

Luke 10:33 But a certain Samaritan, as he journed came where he was ; and when he saw him, he had compassion on him.

Luke 10:37 And he said, He that shewed mercy on him. Then said Jesus unto him " Go, and do thou likewise".

"Staying Plugged in"

As we grow up and respond to the worlds' beckoning call,

We seek peer acceptance, parental guidance, love or nothing at all.

With all of the confusion of life, Gods' word often does not fit into the plan,

It seems that only the desires for personal accumulations are in high demand.

However, just as we need regular contact with our jobs to stay in the race,

We need to daily consult him for hope and love while we seek his face.

Realizing that if we want the constant confusion, stress and hypertension to cease,

That it only through our relationship with him that we will receive the promised peace.

John 15:4 "I am the true vine and ye are the branches"-good fruit- so abide in me

Speaks to our need to stay connected and remain a part of the tree.

When our journey seems to get long and we are experiencing doubt,

Our daily conversations with him, provide us with the necessary clout.

To pretend to be listening, or doing so whenever it is expedient,

Will not impress him, because we are not being obedient.

He will not ignore us and overlook things when we are blatant with sin

So for heveanly instructions and commands,our best advice is "Staying Plugged In"

Richard Lyons

" The Soliloquies (Reflections) Of God"

Luke 15: 11 And he said , a certain man had two sons,

Luke 15 : 13 And not many days after the younger son gathered all

> *together and took his journey into a far country ,and*

> *there wasted his substance with riotous living.*

Luke 15: 17 And when he came to himself, he said, How many hired servants

> *of my father's have bread enough to spare, and I perish with hunger.*

Luke 15: 18 I will arise and go to my father , and I will say to him, Father, I have

> *sinned against heaven and before thee.*

Luke 15 : 19 And no more worthy to be called thy son: make me as one of thy

> *hired servants.*

Luke : 15: 20 And he arose and came to his father. But when he was yet a

> *great way off, his father saw him, and had compassion, and*

> *ran and kissed him.*

Luke 15: 24 For this my son was dead ,and is alive again; he was lost and is found,

> *And they began to be merry.*

"Following Our Faith"

Now faith is the substance of things hoped for and the evidence of things not seen,

This requires spiritual concentration, because physical reality is not very keen.

So to even start our relationship with God, get committed and to begin to achieve,

We have to understand our very creation and in him 1ˢᵗ, start to believe.

Even in biblical times, the revelation of faith was stark

When Noah used it, gained favor with God, then built the ark.

Gods' covenant with us was an agreement that was sure to bind,

So searching diligently for something similar on earth, we will never find.

To believe what God says every time we hear it,

Takes us away from the flesh and put's emphasis on the spirit

Continually embracing his trust from childhood until when we are grown,

Contributes to constantly building our relationship, for that's' where seeds are sown.

Thus, continuing to read his word and believing in his trust,

We begin to understand what his commandments really mean, and do what we must.

To also know that he will take care of our every need,

Is to rekindle our belief in him and have the "Faith of a Mustard Seed"

Richard Lyons

" The Soliloquies (Reflections) Of God"

Matthew 1: 18 Now the birth of Jesus Christ was on the wise; When his mother

Mary was espoused to Joseph, before they came together, she was

found with child of the holy ghost.

Matthew1: 23 Behold, a virgin shall be with child, and shall bring forth a son, and

They shall call his name Emanuel, which being interpreted is God

with us.

Matthew 1: 24 Then Joseph being raised from sleep, did what the angel of the Lord

Bidden him,and took unto him his wife.

Matthew 1: 25 And knew her not till she had brought forth her first born son:

and he called his name Jesus.

" Life's Crooked Paths"

Starting out in life in innocence and with spiritual blinders on too,

Causes our direction to be uncertain, and our paths uncertain in all we do.

Sometimes, perhaps for friendship sake, we are influenced by our peers,

Then, worldly satisfaction as we grow over the years.

Some of us even take illegal and sinful routes to fame,

Then we realize that this way only leads us to ultimate confusiom and shame.

Others of us seemingly take the safe trail, as we pursue higher education,

However, all of us, if we are truthful, come to the same realization.

The roads are full of detours as we continue to march along,

So we change our sinful direction, and continue to sing our song.

Even though some roads are bumpy, and call for us to yield,

We ignore and speed up, because that is the way we feel.

Some, experience worldly success but are still very unfulfilled,

This remains until the desire for idol worship is stilled.

Eventually, getting on the right road and staying on it's path,

Promises to be eternally fruitful. "Now you do the math"

Richard Lyons

" The Soliloquiies (Reflections) Of God

Matthew 28:36 Then cometh Jesus with them unto a place called Gethsemene

and saith unto his disciples, " Sit here while I go and pray yonder"

Matthew 26: 37 And he took with him Peter and the two sons of Zebedee and began

to be sorrowful and very heavy.

Matthew 26:38 Then he said unto them, " My soul is exceedingly sorrowful, even

unto death: tarry ye here, and watch with me.

Matthew 26: 39 And he went a little further, and fell on his face, and prayed

Saying 'O my father , if it be possible, let this cup pass from me:

nevertheless not as I will, but as thou wilt."

Matthew 26:40 And he cometh unto the disciples, and findeth them asleep, and

saith unto Peter " What could you not watch with me for one hour" ?

Matthew 26 :41 Watch and pray, that ye enter not into temptation: the spirit indeed

Is willing, but the flesh is weak.

Matthew 26 : 42 He went away again the second time, and prayed, saying " O my

Father, if this cup may not pass away from me, except I drink it

thy will be done.

"Are We"

Immediate—Expedient— Obedient

In this world, we have to get accustomed to all the speed,

The goal seems to be to got everything we want ,and not just what we need.

We sometimes forget about humbleness and our humility to bow,

As we overlook the weak and poor ,because we strive to have it all now.

Because of man's brain, his technology and his ability to plan,

We overlook the needy simply because we can.

Sometimes the rewards and praise going to the rich and talented is overemphasized.

All because there is no voice of protest coming from the disenfranchised

Certaintly, with all of the instructions and guidelines that come from above

Are we still being neighborly,and careful to show our concern and love?

There is always sickness, poverty, starvation and still,

We sometimes use our human ways of reason to keep from doing his will.

In our final look at things, are we becoming blinded by our desire to achieve?

Or, do we need to reflect back on the fate of adam and eve.

It seems that world domination is the goal for today.

Could it be, that with all of the distractions, we have forgotten to obey?

Richard Lyons

"The Soliloquies (Reflections) Of God"

John 20 :1 The first day of the week cometh Mary Magdalene early when

It was yet dark, unto the sepulcher, and seeth the stone taken away

From the sepulchre.

John 20: 12 And seeth two angels in white sitting, one at the head and the other

at the feet, where the body of Jesus had lain.

John 20: 13 And they say unto her, woman, why weepest thou ? she said unto them,

Because they have taken away my Lord, and I know not where they have

laid him.

John 20:14 And when she had thus said, she turned herself back , and saw Jesus

standing, and knew it was Jesus.

John 20:15 Jesus saith to her , "Woman why weepest thou ?" whom seekest Thou?"

John 20: 16 Jesus saith to her Mary! She turned herself, and saith to him "Rabboni

which is to say Master.

John 20:17 Jesus said unto her, "Touch me not for I am not yet ascended to my fath

But I go to my brethren and say unto them, I ascend unto my father and

Your father, and to my God, and your God.

John20 :23 Whose soever sins ye remit, they are remitted unto them: and

Whose soever sins ye retain, they are retained.

" His persistent voice——Our personal choice"

His voice is compelling to all that will hear it,

Telling us to to convert, repent and begin to worship in the spirit.

The urge may sound like whispers that come from above,

But as you read his word, you begin to feel his covenant of love.

Through his messengers, each day his name will be spread,

For us Christ gave his life and yes, his blood was shed.

Should we continue with satan who will leave our lives in a mess?

Or let Jesus come into our lives and see the changes as he begins to bless.

With his consistent, tender and compassionate cry,

He continues to relay his message to you and I.

Wheras a large number of us will turn a deaf ear,

Some will even put on their Sunday camouflage and pretend not to hear.

Because he is so forgiving, loving and kind,

He is persistently patient, waiting while we make up our minds.

Yes, if we continue in his word he even gives us the expectations,

For he even details the events that will happen in the chapter of revelations.

Richard Lyons

" The Soliloquies (Reflections) Of God"

Luke 23: 26 And as they led him away, they laid hold upon one Simon, a
Cyrenian, coming out of the country, and on him they laid the
cross, that he might bear it after Jesus.

Lule 23:27 And there followed him a great company of people, and of
women, which also bewailed and lamented him.

Luke 23: 28 But Jesus turning unto them said: " Daughters of Jerusalem
weep not for me, but weep for yourselves and for your children.

Luke 23: 29 For , behold the day are coming for which they shall say,
blessed are the barren , and the wombs that never bare, and
the paps which never gave suck.

Luke 23:30 Then shall they begin to say to the mountains "Fall on us"
And to the hills "Cover us".

Luke 23 : Then said Jesus, " Father, forgive them: for they know what they do"

Luke 23:46 And when Jesus had cried out with a loud voice, he said:
"Father, into thy hands I commend my spirit"

" The Certainty of our Uncertainty"

While every human being wonders whether they will eventually endure,

We continue to put flesh over spirit. For we are still unsure.

As we use our minds , we put a premium on our opinion

However, since the beginning of time, God has had total dominion.

In God's holy bible , he has made it clear in the reading of his word,

But most of us continue our way of life, as if we never heard.

As we continue to procrastinate, and wallow in our sorrow,

There will be dire consequences when his judgement comes tomorrow.

We change friends, jobs, locations because this world is vast,

But without a commitment to God, personal satisfaction will not last.

In our stubbornness and because of adulthood, we reluctantly choose,

As a result of our uncertaintly, we continue to lose.

The decision to worship in the spirit should be our ultimate choice,

For , although we can't see him, we certaintly have heard his voice

Yes, judgement day will most certaintly arrive,

Then we will have to give an account of his commands, while we were alive.

Richard Lyons

"The Soliloquies (Reflections) Of God

1st Corinthians 13 :2 And though I have the gift of prophesy, and understand all

  mysteries, and all knowledge: and though I have all faith, so

  that I can remove mountains, and have not charity,I am nothing.

1st Corinthians 1 3;3 And though I bestow all my goods to feed the poor, and though

  I give my body to be burned,and have not charity,it profiteth me

  Nothing.

1st Corinthians 13: 4 Charity suffereth long, and is kind, Charity envieth not, Charity

  vaunteth not itself, is not puffed up.

1st Corinthians 13 :8 Charity never faileth: but whether there be prophecies, they sh

  fail : where there be tongues, they shall cease: where there be

  knowledge, it shall vanish away.

1st Corinthians 13:13 And now abideth " Faith, Hope, Charity, these three: but the

  greatest of these is Charity".

'The Lure vs the cure"

(The Lure) To stay sinful with satan and continue to explore.

(The Cure)   To remain steadfast with Jesus and continue to ignore.

(The Lure) To begin to worship idols because of what you heard.

(The Cure). To be loyal to Jesus and continue to read his word.

(The Lure) To Become sinful and take the worldly bait.

(The Cure) Stay committed to Jesus, obey him and wait.

(The Lure).Remain sinful because it is expedient.

(The Cure) Continue to trust Jesus and remain obedient

(The Lure) Get lost in worldly confusion.

(The Cure). Stay focused on him and keep your eyes on the final conclusion.

(The Lure) Ger drawn into drugs and take your chances with the pill.

(The Cure) Solidify your loyalty to him and continue to do his will.

(The Lure) Continue to let satan tempt and scheme.

(The Cure) Hold on to his promise and let him redeem.

(The Lure) Remain sinful and plugged into the worldly cast.

(The Cure) Stay true to him and remain steadfast.

(The Lure) Living in this world,you will certaintly be open to the lure

(The Cure) However, with Jesus as your companion, nothing compares to the cure.

Richard Lyons

"The Soliloquies(Reflection) Of God"

2nd John :2 For the truths sake which dwellenth in us , and shall be with us

    for ever.

2nd John: 3 Grace be with you, mercy, and peace, from God the father, and

    from the Lord Jesus Christ, the son of the father, in truth and love.

2nd John:4 I rejoiced that I found of thy children walking in truth, as we have

    a commandment from the father.

2nd John : 5 And now I beseech the , lady not as though I wrote a new commandme

    unto thee, but that which we had from the beginning, that we love one

    another.

2nd John: 6 And this is love , that we walk after his commandments, That, as ye

    have heard from the beginning, ye should walk in it.

2nd John: 9 Whosoever transgreseth, and abide not in the doctrine of Christ

    hath not God. He that abide not in the doctrine of Christ, He hath

    both the father and the son.

" Our Opportunity For Immunity"

\

To start each day, we all have a golden chance,

We could improve our relationship with him and receive a favorable glance.

Although sometimes uncertain, we could state our pleas,

Then, with a show humbleness and humility, gently fall on our knees.

Whether our daily travels be by automobile, air, or commuter train,

If we are vigilant, there . may be chances to show love and compassion to ease the pain.

We all could let go of the coldness and aloofness for a little while,

Then replace them with love and concern and yes, show a godly smile.

Although, to show love and compassion might be a rarity,

It is one of God's given traits, so we should willingly show our charity.

There sometimes even may be a good reason to resist,

However, if we continue to be vigilant, we can find ways to persist.

Consequently, we all have God in us, if we put away our pride,

So we should always show love and charity because these traits we should not hide.

Yes,if each of us becomes more vigilant for God, we could sing the same tune,

For by doing his will, we could all become more obedient and eternally immune.

Richard Lyons

" The Soliloquies (Reflections) Of God"

Hebrews 10: 16 This is the covenant that I make with them after those days,
saith the Lord, I will put my laws into their hearts, and in their
minds will I write them.

Hebrews :10:17 And their sins and iniquities will I remember no more.

Hebrews 10 : 18 Now where remission of these is, there is no more offering of
sin.

Hebrews 10: 26 For if we sin willfully after that, we have received the knowledge
of the truth, there remaineth no more sacrifice for sin.

Hebrews 10: 29 Of how much sorer punishment suppose ye, shall he be thought
worthy? Who have trodden under foot the son of God and hath
counted the blood of the covenant, wherewith he was sanctified,
an unholy thing, hath done despite unto the spirit of grace.

Hebrews 10 :30 For we know him that hath said " Vengence belongeth to me, I
Will Recompense" saith the Lord, and again The Lord shall judge h
People.

The Cover of Night
VS
The Lover Of Light

It seems that as daylight fades and gives way to night,

Then that is the signal for evil doers to partner with satan and begin their plight.

The acceleration of sin is apparent as they attack one another,

They seem to willfully ignore god's command to love their brother.

However, God said that he is light, and in him there is no darkness at all,

We are reminded that he did not give us the spirit of fear, so be vigilant to his call.

He want's us to continue to press on through the day and night,

To be strong and continue to spread his word, and not show any fright.

Although, the level of opportunity seems to increase when it's dark,

If we are are securely grounded in him, our heavenly control will make it's mark.

Yes, sinful activity will continue ,and will always be,

Just remember, that God is light, and to abide in him , is all the light we need to see.

So, as man is exposed to sin whether it's day or night,

The key is to remain close to Jesus and always walk in his light.

Even with the cover of night ,when the tall buildings and such camaflauge wicked men

Evildoers will not be able to hide, for God will still be able to detect their sin.

Richard Lyons

" The Soliloquies (Reflections) Of God"

Revelations 2:2 I know thy works, and thy labour, and thy patience, and how

      thou canst not bear them that are evil: and thou hast tried them

      which say they are apostles, and are not and hast found them liars,

Revelations 2: 5 Remember, therefore from whence thou have fallen, and repent

      and do the first works; or else I will come unto thee quickly, and

      will remove thy candlestick out of his place, except thou repent!

Revelations 2: 11 He that hath an ear, let him hear what the spirit saith unto the

      churches: He that overcometh shall not be hurt of the second death.

Revelations 2: 16 Repent: or else I will come quickly and will fight against them

      with the sword of my mouth.

Revelations 2: 17 He that hath an ear, let him hear what the spirit saith unto the

      churches; To him that overcometh, will I give to eat of the living

      manna, and will give him a white stone, and in the stone a new

      name written , which no man knoweth saving he that recieveth it.

Revelations 2: 19 I know thy works, and charity, and service and faith and thy

      patience , and thy works: and the last to be more than the first

"Things"

Some things never come back like "words" uttered and the presence of "time",

But, the truthful words of God remain strong, for they are sublime.

Other things that can destroy a person are "anger", "unforgiveness" and "pride",

So, asking God for repentance of these is a request we should not hide.

Also, things that we should never lose in life are "hope", "honesty" and "peace",

For when we are grounded in him, worldly frustrations begin to cease.

Yes, while the things that are most valuable in life are "kindness", "family" and "love"

We know of their worth because they came from above.

The most fleeting things in life are "fortune", "dreams" and "success",

However, God shows us how to put things in prospective, while he continues to bless.

Now, the things that make a person are "hard work", "sincerity" & ability to" "commit"

But, these are human qualities of judgment whether we ride, stand or sit.

The most important things are "Jesus", "sacrifice" and the "word"

Then, to begin to understand, be thankful and respond to what we've heard.

Now, the things that are truly constant, whenever we hear it,
                    Are the
        Father——Son——Holy Spirit

Richard Lyons

44

" Our Vanity Or God's Sanity"

When we look at the total sacrifice made for us by him on the cross,

For us to deny his deep love and continue to express our vanity is false.

Even in our daily conversation, when we take the Lord thy God in vain,

Our God is awesome enough to hear, and this causes him much pain.

To put on a daily sin – free face for the world, makes it easy to deceive,

However, it is the full repentance from God that we need to receive.

Satan will cause you to feel that you are on top, but you are really on the brink,

But , the voice and presence of Jesus, will make you stop and think.

We need to practice love and vigilance in Christ each and every day,

Thus, if we ignore the constant influences of sin, he will bless us in every way.

Also, when we send up a generic prayer, it is just an illusion,

For it needs to be real, loving and meaningful, otherwise it causes spiritual confusion.

It is not important to him, how much we embrace technology,or keep a worldly journal,

Only our commitment to follow his commands, will it result in life eternal.

We should always remember, when Satan is around, he makes it seem very real,

However, there is no comparison to the way the holy spirit can make you feel.

Richard Lyons

45

MORNING ON THE SEA OF GALILEE

46

The
Right   Direction
Toward
God's   Protection

The directional traffic lights of green, amber and red,

Could be compared to our Jesus Christ, and the blood that he shed.

To observe the yellow and show caution with the way we are living,

Then to obey the green as an urge from him is to continue charitable giving.

There are repeated commands from him for us to go the right way,

But most of us take the detour, find a dead end, then have to correct our stray.

Our lives become all tangled and we get in a rut,

Because we become disobedient in thinking that we can take the short cut.

The right way is to stay connected, for he says that he is the vine,

He says for us to forget worldly success, for : "victory will be mine"

When we start off with him as babies, we may begin on the floor,

But as we travel the road to eternity,he says you must come in through the door.

Once you are traveling on the right road, you can't be a quitter,

So, use God as your navigator, then activate facebook and twitter.

Your relationship with him will keep you on the right track,

Because, once you are plugged in, you will not want turn back.

Richard Lyons

SHEPHERDS IN BETHLEHEM

" It's Later Than You Think"

God didn't just intend for the message in revelations to be read by some,

He intended for the events and the eternal prize to be available to all who overcome.

He said that he was the alpha ,the omega, the beginning and the end,

His judgement day will reap havoc, especially for those who have not repented their sin

There will be much wrath and affliction for those whose intent was to rob,steal and kill

He will certainly separate them from the ones that were always ready, to do his will.

We go through this world everyday in constant comfusion,

However, if we are wise, we need to quickly prepare ourselves, for the final conclusion.

In 1ˢᵗ Thessalonians 5:2 The Lord says that he will come as a thief in the night,

Thus , without any warning, our readiness and repentance should be right.

We should also take heed, the warning signs with each natural disaster.

For the signals of judgement day, come straight from the master.

On a worldwide basis, his prediction of wars and rumors of wars has come of age,

Man on a universal basis, seem unable to control his rage.

So,with all of the sin that is occurring, we are certaintly on the brink,

Therefore with our intelligence,we should know: "It is later than we think"

Richard Lyons

THE WAILING WALL IN JERUSALEM

" The Total Price"

Yes Jesus lived his life and when he died he was only thirty three,

He was tortured, he suffered and he paid the price for you and me.

There ,on Calvary,he was led to the cross by the Romans. Then- crucified.

But Jesus was on a mission and it was for you and I, that he died.

Before, there was the apostle Judas, who was the one to betray,

However, for the sacrifice he paid for us, we could never repay.

They drove nails through his tendons in order to inflict much pain,

The blood left his body, flowing from his arteries and veins.

After his death, his beloved followers searched for his burial site until detection,

But when they came to his grave , they discovered his resurrection.

Thus, it became true that with all of the torture and pain,

That it was a fact, with out any doubt,like prophesized, that he would rise again.

Jesus died for all of us, citing repentance and remission of sin,

Saying that only through him, could we reach eternity, and win.

He finally admonished us continue to spread his name and spread the good news,

So, we should strive to avoid doing evil and avoid satan, for we are sure to lose.

Richard Lyons

MARKETPLACE IN THE HOLY LAND

" Living The Good Life"

To be deemed successful on a worldly scale, you have to have money and status,

However, in God's eyesight, it's not your finances or worldly rank that really matters.

It is our response to the mournful cries of the poor that we should take heed,

You see, it is far more impressive to God, when we actually respond to their need.

When we are able to show thanks and gratitude at the start of each day,

It also is a bonus when we receive God's guidance as we go along the way.

Plus, to avoid personal illness and sin while evil doers are being stressed,

Is to remain thankful and vigilant and continue to be blessed.

Being loving and compassionate with our neighbors when we show them that we care,

Yes, we become doers of his word, when we show that we are willing to share.

Then when we can lead others to Christ we show them the meaning of real fame,

Because then we are responding to God's covenant to continue to spread his name.

If, each day we can escape satan's persistent wrath,

We can continually praise God's name, because we are on the right path.

To continue to keep his commandments, be vigilant and learn to conquer real strife.

As sin and disobedience decreases, we will be " Living the Good Life"

Richard Lyons

JERUSALEM FROM THE MOUNT OF OLIVES

In Conclusion

It is my sincere hope that your reading of the previous pages was enjoyable and fulfilling to you. Also that you were able to use some of these as comparison points in your Christian life. The opportunity to share his name is one of the things that God wants us to do. So, let' continue to be obedient to him in all that we do. May God continue to bless you and may his hand of guidance be with you the remainder of your way through.

"GOD BLESS"